Bible

VOLUME TWO

For:

_____

From:

_____

Date:

_____

My people, listen to my teaching.
    Listen to what I say.
I will speak using stories.
    I will tell things that have been
    secret since long ago.
We have heard them and know them.
    Our fathers told them to us.
We will not keep them from our children.
    We will tell those who come later
    about the praises of the Lord.
We will tell about his power
    and the miracles he has done.

PSALM 78: 1–4

THE ULTIMATE DVD READ AND SHARE® Bible

VOLUME TWO

More Than 100 Best-Loved
Bible Stories

Stories Retold by
Gwen Ellis

Illustrated by Steve Smallman

Tommy NELSON®

A Division of Thomas Nelson Publishers

NASHVILLE   DALLAS   MEXICO CITY   RIO DE JANEIRO

The Ultimate DVD Read and Share® Bible Volume Two
© 2007, 2010 by Tommy Nelson, a Division of Thomas Nelson, Inc.

Published in Nashville, Tennessee, by Tommy Nelson.
Tommy Nelson is a registered trademark of Thomas Nelson, Inc.

Stories based on *The Holy Bible, International Children's Bible*®, copyright © 1986, 1988, 1999, 2005 by Thomas Nelson, Inc.

Stories retold by Gwen Ellis
Illustrated by Steve Smallman

Tommy Nelson titles may be purchased in bulk for educational, business, fund-raising, or sales promotional use. For information, please e-mail SpecialMarkets@ThomasNelson.com.

ISBN 978-1-4003-1614-4 (Volume Two)

The Library of Congress has cataloged the earlier printing as follows:
Ellis, Gwen.
    Read and share Bible : more than 200 best-loved Bible stories / by Gwen Ellis.
      p. cm.
    ISBN 978-1-4003-0853-8 (hardback)
    1. Bible stories, English. I. Title.
  BS551.3.E55 2007
  220.9'505—dc22   2006029401

Mfr.: RR Donnelley / Shenzhen, China / January 2011 / PPO # 116030

Stories on DVD 1

Joseph the Slave—*Joseph's Dreams; Joseph's Coat; Joseph is Sold*

Joseph in Jail—*Joseph Explains Dreams; The Baker's Dream; The King's Dream*

Joseph in Charge—*Joseph's Brothers Visit Egypt; Spies!*

Joseph and His Brothers—*Bowing Brothers; Joseph Tricks His Brothers; Jacob in Egypt*

Moses—*A Mean King; A Baby Boy; Good Sister; A Royal Princess; Moses' Real Mother Helps*

Strange Fire—*Moses Runs Away; Strange Fire; Moses Goes Home*

Moses Goes Home—*The Kings Says No!; A Mistake?; The Walking Stick Miracle*

Moses Parts the Water—*Cloud and Fire; Trapped at the Red Sea; A Dry Path*

Ten Commandments—*Food and Water; The Mountaintop*

Balaam's Donkey—*The Donkey and the Angel*

The First Lord's Supper—*Jesus Borrows a Donkey; Jesus Rides Like a King; How to Serve*

Jesus' Resurrection—*Jesus is Alive!; Jesus with Two Friends; Jesus Goes to Heaven*

The Holy Spirit Comes—*God's Spirit Comes to Help; Everyone Hears and Understands; A Beggar at the Temple*

Stories on DVD 2

The Promised Land—*Crossing Jordan; The Walls of Jericho; The Sun Stands Still*

Solomon—*The Wisest Man; Whose Baby?*

Elisha—*Seven Dips in the Jordan River*

Daniel—*Writing on the Wall; Daniel Disobeys the King; A Den of Hungry Lions*

Jonah—*Jonah Runs Away; A Big Storm; Jonah Goes Overboard; Inside a Big Fish*

Where Is Jesus?—*Jesus with the Temple Teachers*

Jesus Walks on the Water

Jesus' Life—*A Very Poor Woman; Jesus Stops a Storm*

Jesus' Power—*Jesus' Best Friends; One Man Says Thank You*

Jesus' Life—*A Coin in a Fish; A Blind Man Sees Again; Jesus Brings Lazarus Back to Life*

Philip—*Philip Meets an Ethiopian; Philip Baptizes the Ethiopian*

Peter—*Peter in Jail*

The Best Is Yet to Come—*New Heaven and Earth; A Promise to All God's Children*

Contents

New Testament Stories 144

Old Testament

Joseph's Dreams

Genesis 37:1-8

Joseph had 11 brothers. His father was Jacob. He loved all his sons, but he loved Joseph best. Joseph liked to tell his brothers about his dreams. He said, in one dream, all 12 brothers had bundles of wheat.

Then he said 11 bundles bowed down to his bundle. Oooo! That made the older brothers mad. "You're not the king over us," they told him.

God had a plan for this family that no one could see yet. God has a plan for your family too.

Joseph's Coat

Jacob gave Joseph a beautiful coat with long sleeves. This made his brothers jealous.

One day Jacob said, "Joseph, go check on your brothers." So off Joseph went. His brothers saw him coming. "Here comes the dreamer," they said. "Let's get rid of him." Watch out, Joseph!

**Those brothers were up to no good.
What would they do to Joseph?**

Joseph Is Sold

Genesis 37:21–28

The brothers hated Joseph. But one of them said, "Let's not hurt him. Let's just throw him down this well." He planned to rescue Joseph later. So they took off Joseph's coat and threw him in.

About that time, some men on camels rode by. "Hey," the brothers said, "let's sell him to be a slave." They sold their own brother.

What the brothers did was awful.
What would happen next?

Joseph the Slave

Genesis 39:1–6

Joseph was not alone. God was watching over him. Soon a rich man named Potiphar bought him to be his slave. Joseph worked and did great at everything Potiphar asked him to do.

So Potiphar put Joseph in charge of his whole house, and everyone had to do what Joseph said.

Even when things look bad, God is watching over His children. He's watching over you right now.

Joseph in Jail

Genesis 39:6–20

Everything was going great for Joseph, until one day Potiphar's wife tried to trick him. She told lies about Joseph, and Potiphar believed her.

Potiphar threw Joseph into jail. Poor Joseph. His brothers sold him, a lady lied about him, and he was thrown into jail. It wasn't fair. But God had a plan for Joseph.

Lots of things happen to us that aren't fair. But, remember, God always has a plan to help us.

Joseph Explains Dreams

Genesis 40:1–13, 20–21

In the prison, one of the prisoners told Joseph about a dream he'd had. Joseph listened carefully, and God showed him what the man's dream meant.

12

Joseph said that in three days the man would be working for the king of Egypt like he had before being put in prison. Sure enough, that's exactly what happened.

Joseph knew what God could do. He had learned how to listen to God. You can too.

The Baker's Dream

Genesis 40:16–22

Another prisoner dreamed he had three baskets of bread that he had baked for the king. In his dream the birds kept eating up all the bread.

Joseph didn't have very good news about this dream. He said, "In three days you will die." Joseph told the truth.

Why do you think Joseph was so good at telling what dreams meant? The most important dream Joseph would hear about was just ahead.

The King's Dream

Genesis 41:1–36

One night the king of Egypt dreamed that seven skinny cows came from the river and ate up seven fat cows. No one could figure out what the dream meant.

"Call for Joseph," said the first man who had told Joseph his dream in the prison. They did, and God showed Joseph what the king's dream meant. There would be seven years with lots of food. Then there would be seven years with almost no food.

That was a scary dream, wasn't it? Sometimes our dreams mean something, and sometimes they are just dreams.

Joseph
in Charge

Genesis 41:37–43

When the king heard what Joseph said, he did something amazing. He put Joseph in charge of gathering enough food to feed everyone during the hungry time.

The king took off his royal ring and put it on Joseph's finger. He gave Joseph fine clothes to wear and put a gold chain around his neck. The king had Joseph ride in one of the royal chariots, and everyone had to bow down to him.

Joseph went from being a prisoner in the morning to a ruler in the afternoon. That was because God had a plan for Joseph and his family.

Joseph's Brothers Visit Egypt

Genesis 41:46–42:6

For the next seven years, Joseph stored lots of food. Then the hungry time came. It was bad for other lands, but the people of Egypt had food.

Joseph's family, back home, were very hungry. "Go to Egypt and buy grain," Jacob told his sons. So ten brothers packed up and went to Egypt. The youngest brother, Benjamin, stayed home.

Whoa! What do you think the brothers will do when they see Joseph?

Spies!

Genesis 42:7–20

When the brothers came to the palace, Joseph knew right away who they were. But they didn't recognize him.

"You're spies," he said to test them. They replied, "No, we've come to buy food." They told Joseph all about their family.

Joseph gave them food but said if they ever came back they must bring their youngest brother.

Joseph wanted to see Benjamin. What do you think the brothers were thinking? Do you think they'll bring Benjamin next time?

23

The Bowing Brothers

Genesis 43:15–26

One day Joseph's brothers needed more food. They came back to Egypt and brought Benjamin with them. Joseph told his servants to prepare a feast for them.

When Joseph came to the feast, all the brothers bowed down to him. It was just like Joseph's dream about his brothers' bundles of wheat bowing down to his.

Do you think Joseph's dream had come true?

Joseph Tricks His Brothers

Genesis 43:29–44:13

When Joseph saw Benjamin, he was so happy, he began to cry. But he didn't let anyone see his tears. Joseph gave the brothers the grain they wanted.

But he tricked them. He put his cup in Benjamin's sack. The rule was that whoever took something from the ruler had to be his servant forever. Benjamin couldn't go home.

Joseph tricked his brothers because he wanted to see if their hearts had changed or if they would let someone take another brother.
What would happen next?

Jacob Goes to Egypt

Genesis 44:3–45:28

The brothers begged Joseph not to keep Benjamin. Joseph saw that their hearts had changed. He said, "I am your brother Joseph. You sold me to be a slave, but God sent me here to save your lives."

"Hurry, go home and get our father and your families and bring them here." And that's how God's people, the Israelites, came to live in Egypt.

God always has a plan. He has a plan for you too.

A Mean King

Exodus 1:8–14

Years later, long after Joseph died, a mean king made the Israelites his slaves. The slave masters were mean too. They made the Israelites work harder and harder to make bricks and do other things for the king.

"There are too many Israelites, and they are too strong," said the king. So he thought up an awful thing to do.

Why do you think the king was mean to the Israelites?

A Baby Boy

Exodus 1:22–2:2

That mean old king said, "Every time an Israelite baby boy is born, you must throw him into the river." That was terrible!

32

One day an Israelite woman had a beautiful baby boy. She decided to hide her baby from the evil king and his helpers. It was a good choice.

When we make the right choice, God always helps us. Let's see what happened next.

The Good Sister

Exodus 2:3–4

After a while the baby's mother couldn't hide him anymore. So she got a basket and fixed it so the water could not get inside.

Then she put the baby into the basket and put the basket into the river. The baby's big sister, Miriam, stayed close by to see what would happen.

Miriam must have been very frightened. What do you think she said when she prayed for her little brother?

A Princess Finds Moses

Exodus 2:5–10

God was watching over the baby. When the princess came to the river to take a bath, she saw the basket. "Go get that basket," she told her servant.

The princess looked inside the basket. Just then the baby cried, and she felt sorry for him. The princess decided to keep him as her son. She named him Moses.

This was exciting! Moses was going to be a prince of Egypt. But something even better was about to happen.

Moses' Real Mother Helps

Exodus 2:7–10

Miriam was still watching. Even though she was frightened, she stepped out and asked, "Do you need someone to take care of the baby?" The princess smiled. "Why, yes," she replied.

Miriam ran home and got her mother—
Moses' own mother—to take care of
him. God saved Baby Moses and gave
him back to his mother for a long time.

Many exciting things were going to happen
to Moses when he grew up. Let's read on.

Moses Runs Away

Exodus 2:11–3:3

After a while Moses went to the palace to live. When he was grown up, Moses did something very bad. He killed another man.

Moses ran away to live in the desert. He married a lady named Zipporah. Her father's name was Jethro. One day when Moses was out with the sheep, he saw a bush in the desert. It was on fire, but it didn't burn up.

What was going on? Why didn't the bush burn up?

Strange Fire

Exodus 3:4–12

Moses went to look at this strange fire. God spoke
to Moses from the fire. "Don't come any closer.
Take off your sandals. You are on holy ground."
Moses was scared. He covered his face. "Go, bring
My people out of Egypt," God said.

"I can't do that," Moses said. But God promised to help Moses lead the people.

Whenever God asks us to do hard things, He will help us. Let's see how He helped Moses.

43

Moses Goes Home

Exodus 4:14–5:1

Moses went home to Egypt to talk to the Israelites about being free. God sent Moses' brother Aaron to help him.

44

The Israelites fell right down on their knees and thanked God for remembering them. Then it was time for Moses to go see the mean king. Moses took Aaron with him.

Oh my! Moses had to ask the king to let all those people go free. What do you think the king said?

The King Says No!

Exodus 5:1–9

Moses walked right up to the king and said, "God says, 'Let My people go!'" The king said, "I don't know your God. Why should I obey Him? These people have work to do. They cannot leave."

46

Then the king made the people work even harder. What a mean man! This made the Israelite leaders angry with Moses.

Do you think Moses had made a mistake?

A Mistake?

Exodus 5:19–6:9

The Israelite leaders were angry. They thought Moses had surely made a big mistake. "You made the king hate us," they said.

Moses talked to God. "Lord, why have You brought this trouble on the people? Is this why You sent me here?" God answered, "You will see what I will do to the king."

Sometimes even when we do good, things get worse for a while. This is when we need to remember that God can see ahead.

The Walking-Stick Miracle

Exodus 7:8–13

God sent Moses and Aaron back to the king. "Let God's people go," Moses said. "Do a miracle," said the king. Aaron threw down his walking stick, and it became a snake.

50

The king's magicians threw down their sticks, and they became snakes too. But Aaron's snake swallowed them all. God's power was the strongest. Still the king was so evil and his heart was so hard that he said, "No, your people cannot leave."

This is just getting harder and harder. How will God rescue His people?

A River Turns to Blood

Exodus 7:14–24

God said to Moses, "Go meet the king at the river. Tell him to let My people go, or I will turn this river into blood." Of course, the king said no. So Aaron hit the water with his walking stick, and the river turned to blood.

It smelled awful, and there was no water for the people to drink.

Sometimes people don't want to listen to God. What else do you think will happen to that stubborn king?

Frogs, Frogs, Frogs

Exodus 7:25–8:15

After seven days Moses went back to the king. "Let God's people go," said Moses. "No," said the king.

This time God sent frogs. Not just one or two, but more than anyone could count! The frogs went in the houses, in the beds, in the food, and in the ovens. The frogs were icky, and they were everywhere.

God meant business. How much worse do you think it will get before the king says yes?

Gnats, Flies, and Boils

Exodus 8:16–9:12

Every time the king said no, things just went from bad to worse in Egypt. God sent little bitty gnats that crawled all over the people.

Next He sent millions of flies. They were everywhere. Cows got sick and died. Then people got sick with big sores called *boils*. But the king still said no each time.

That king sure was stubborn! Can you guess what awful thing came next?

Hail, Locusts, and Darkness

Exodus 9:13–10:29

Next God sent a storm. Big chunks of ice called *hail* pounded every plant into the ground. Then hungry grasshoppers called *locusts* blew in with the wind. There were so many of them, the people couldn't see the ground. The grasshoppers ate all the food.

Then God sent darkness right in the middle of the day. The Egyptians couldn't see anything. But the king still said no.

Why do you think the king kept saying no?

Standing-Up Dinner

Exodus 11:1–12:28

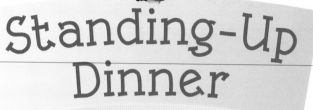

God told His people to fix a dinner of roast lamb and to eat dinner standing up with all their clothes on.

He told them to have their walking sticks in their hands. God knew the king would soon change his mind, and His people needed to be ready to go.

On this night the children got to stay up late and eat dinner with their parents. Tell what you think happened next.

Something Awful

Exodus 12:29–51

At midnight something awful happened in Egypt because the king was so stubborn. All the oldest boys, cows, horses, and other animals died. But not one of God's people or their animals died.

Finally the king said, "Take everything you have and leave Egypt." God's people were free at last!

God didn't want bad things to happen to the people, but He had to make the king listen.

Cloud and Fire

Exodus 13:21–22

When God's people left Egypt, they marched out into the desert. God did something very special to help them. He sent a tall cloud to guide them during the day.

64

It was very dark in the desert at night. So God changed the cloud to fire. It was like a giant night-light. Now God's people could travel some during the day and some at night.

God loved His people. He was taking care of them just like He takes care of us.

Trapped at the Red Sea

Exodus 14:5–14

Back in Egypt the king changed his mind. He sent his army after the Israelites to bring them back. Closer and closer the army of horses and chariots came.

God's people stood right by the Red Sea. There was no way across the water. The king's soldiers were behind them, and the sea was in front of them. It looked as if they were trapped, but they weren't.

**How do you think God's people felt at that moment?
Sad? Scared? Hopeful?**

A Dry Path

Just then God moved the tall cloud
behind His people to hide them from
the enemy. The Egyptians couldn't see
anything. The cloud made it dark for
them. But it gave light to God's people
on the other side of the cloud.

Then Moses raised his hand over the sea. All night God pushed back the sea with a strong wind. And the water split to make a dry path to the other side. The Israelites safely reached the other side. But when the Egyptian army tried to use the same path, the water came back together and covered the soldiers. And that was the end of the king's army.

Can you imagine what it was like to walk on a path in the middle of the sea?

Food and Water

God led His people through the desert. God loved them. He made sure they had plenty of food and water. He gave them a strange, white food called *manna*. It came from the sky and was very good for them, but the people whined and whined.

70

Once God even made water come out of a rock so they would have fresh water to drink. The people were happy to have water. They stopped whining for a little while.

God wants us to be thankful. What are you thankful for? What should you tell God?

Ten Commandments

Exodus 20:2–17; 24:12–18

One day God called Moses up to the top of a mountain to have a talk.

God gave Moses many rules to help His people know how to live. God wrote the rules on stone with His finger. We call these rules *The Ten Commandments*.

God gives us rules to keep us safe. Rules help us live happy lives. Moms and dads have rules too. Can you name one?

A Tent House for God

Exodus 25:8-9; 31:1-11

God had told Moses to build a Holy Tent
so that God could live close to His people.
Then God gave Moses someone to help
him build the Holy Tent.

The helper's name was Bezalel. God said His Spirit would help Bezalel know how to make beautiful things from silver and gold and jewels and carved wood for God's house.

God gives different skills and talents to different people. What do you do best? Have you thanked God for this special talent?

A Holy Box

Exodus 25:10–22; 40:20–21, 34–38

One of the things Bezalel made for the Tent was the Holy Box. He covered the box with pure gold. He made a lid of pure gold too.

Moses put the stones with God's commandments on them inside the Holy Box. Bezalel and Moses worked hard to make everything perfect. When the Holy Tent was finished, God's presence filled it up. God had come to live with His people.

Where do people go to worship God today?

Moses and Joshua

Exodus 33:7–11

Before the Holy Tent was built, Moses would set up another tent outside the camp. When Moses went to the tent to talk with God, he often took a young man named Joshua with him.

All the people stood outside and watched the two men go by. As soon as Moses and Joshua were inside the tent, the tall cloud would come down and cover the doorway.

What do you suppose was going on
inside the tent? Let's see.

Inside the Tent

Exodus 33:11; Joshua 1:1–9

Inside the tent God and Moses talked like old friends, and Joshua listened. This was one of the ways Moses was teaching Joshua how to be a leader of God's people.

When Moses left the tent to go home,
Joshua liked to stay at the tent.

It was important for Joshua to get to know God.
God had lots of work for him to do.

You can get to know God, too, by praying and
listening to what God says in the Bible.

Moses Sees God

Exodus 33:18–23; 34:29–35

One day Moses asked God, "Will You show me how great You are?" God tucked Moses into a crack in a rock and passed in front of him.

Moses only saw God's back. But it was enough. Moses' face became so shiny from being close to God that people couldn't look at him. Moses had to cover his face to keep the light from hurting their eyes.

Wow, Moses really got close to God, didn't he? How do you think we can get close to God?

12 Men Explore

Numbers 13:1–14:35

One day Moses sent 12 men to explore the land God had promised His people. The land had lots of food, but the people who lived there were like giants. Two men, Joshua and Caleb, said, "Don't worry. God is with us, and He is stronger than any giants."

But the other men were afraid and said, "We can't go into the land." God was not happy with His people. They did not trust Him. So God's people had to wander around in the desert 40 more years.

**God wants us to believe His Word.
Of the 12 men who explored the new land,
who were the two that trusted God?**

Balaam's Donkey

Numbers 22:1–22

Close to the end of their time in the desert, all God's people camped near a city. The king of that city was afraid when he saw so many people camped nearby. He sent for a prophet named Balaam. "Do something to make these people go away," he said.

So Balaam started off on his donkey to see what he could do. That made God angry because He wanted His people to be there.

God had a big surprise for Balaam. Turn the page and see what happened.

The Donkey and the Angel

Numbers 22:22–35

God sent an angel with a sword to stop Balaam. Balaam couldn't see the angel, but his donkey could. The donkey stopped. When Balaam beat the donkey to make it go, the donkey said, "Why are you beating me?" Then Balaam saw the angel. The angel told Balaam to help God's people.

God can do anything. He even made a donkey talk so Balaam would pay attention.

Crossing Jordan

Joshua 3

Finally it was time for God's people to go into their new land. But first they had to cross the Jordan River.

There were no bridges or boats. God told the priests to carry the Holy Box and walk into the water. When they did, God made a dry path, and His people walked across to the other side of the river.

What do you think other people thought when they heard what God did for His people?

The Walls of Jericho

Joshua 6

The first city they came to was Jericho. It had huge walls and gates and guards everywhere. God said, "March around Jericho every day for six days. Seven priests with trumpets must march at the front."

"On the seventh day, march around seven times. Then have the priests blow one long blast on their trumpets. The people must shout and the walls will fall down." The people obeyed and down came those walls.

Sometimes God asks us to do things we don't understand. We just need to obey.

The Sun Stands Still

Joshua 10:1–14

Joshua fought hard to win the land
God had promised to His people. And
God helped him. One day God sent huge
hailstones to fall on the enemy.

Later that day the battle was not finished. Joshua said, "Sun, stand still!" God kept the sun right where it was until His people won the battle.

Nothing is impossible when God is on our side. God wants to help us.

The Wisest Man

1 Kings 3:4–15

David was king for forty years. He had many sons. But it was his son Solomon who became king when David died. Solomon knew that wise kings make good decisions. He prayed and asked God to make him wise so that he could understand God's laws. God heard his prayer and made him the wisest man who ever lived.

Any one of us can ask God to make us wise,
and He will. Let's see how Solomon's wisdom
helped two women.

97

Whose Baby?

1 Kings 3:16–28

Two women brought a baby to Solomon. Each woman said the baby was hers. Solomon knew just what to do to find out who the real mother was. He said he could cut the baby in half and give one part to each woman.

But one woman pointed to the other woman and said, "No, don't hurt the baby. Give the baby to her." Then Solomon knew the woman who said this was the real mother.

Solomon wasn't really going to hurt the baby. What was he trying to find out?

Elijah's Coat

2 Kings 2:13–14

As a whirlwind took Elijah the prophet to heaven, his coat fell off and landed on the ground. Another prophet named Elisha picked it up.

He went to the river and hit the water with the coat. He said, "Where is the God of Elijah?" Elisha wanted to see if God's power was on him like it had been on Elijah. It was. The water split in the middle, and Elisha walked across on dry ground.

This was the first miracle God did through Elisha. Keep reading to learn about more miracles that came later.

The Miracle of the Pot of Oil

2 Kings 4:1–7

"My dead husband owed money to a man. That man is going to make my two sons his slaves," a woman told Elisha. "I have nothing but this small pot of oil."

"Get empty jars from your neighbors," said Elisha. "Now pour oil into them." When the woman started pouring oil from her pot, it just kept coming. She filled every jar in the house. Then she sold the oil, paid her debt to the man, and saved her boys from slavery.

How could a small pot of oil fill so many big jars and pots? It was a miracle!

Elisha Helps a Little Boy

2 Kings 4:8–37

Another woman also begged Elisha for help. Her little boy had died. Elisha went to her house.

104

He went to the room where the little boy's body lay and prayed over him. The little boy sneezed and opened his eyes. He had come back to life, and he was just fine.

This was another wonderful miracle. Only God can give people life.

Poison in the Stew

Elisha met some hungry men. He had his servant make them stew. One of the men wanted to help. He found some plants and added them to the stew. He didn't know they were poisonous.

106

When the men started eating, they cried, "There's death in the pot!" Elisha put flour into the stew, and the food became safe to eat.

Throwing flour into a stew doesn't usually remove poison. This was another miracle from God.

Food for Everyone

2 Kings 4:42-44

People all over Israel were running out of food. They were hungry. One man brought 20 loaves of bread to Elisha. Elisha said, "Feed the people." The man said, "We can't feed 100 men with so little bread."

Elisha told him to start feeding them and there would be bread left over. Sure enough, that's what happened!

Elisha was not doing these miracles in his own power. God was helping him. What miracle do you think happened next?

Seven Dips in the Jordan River

2 Kings 5:1–14

Naaman, an important soldier, had a terrible skin disease called *leprosy*. People who had leprosy could not come close to other people. They had to live in lepers' towns. Naaman's wife's servant girl said, "I wish my master could meet Elisha. He would heal him."

So Naaman went to find Elisha. "Wash in the Jordan River seven times, and you'll be healed," Elisha said. Naaman was embarrassed. What Elisha told him to do seemed silly. But he went to the river to wash himself, and on the seventh time the leprosy disappeared.

If a dip in the river would make you well from a terrible sickness, would you do it, even if it seemed silly?

A Floating Ax

2 Kings 6:1–7

Some men were building a meeting house for Elisha. As they were chopping down trees for the house, an ax broke. The metal part fell into the river and sank. The man who was using it yelled, "That was an ax I'd borrowed!"

112

Elisha threw a stick into the water, and the iron ax head floated up.

Wow! Ax heads are heavy and can't float, unless God makes them do it. God can do anything!

113

No Food!

2 Kings 6:24–25; 7:1–9

An army surrounded the city of Samaria, and no one could go in or come out. The people in the city had no food. God told Elisha to say that tomorrow there would be lots of food. About that time four men decided to see if the enemy would give them something to eat. When they got to the camp, there was no one there.

The soldiers had run away, leaving all their food and gold and clothes. At first the men started to hide the treasure for themselves. But then they decided to share. They told the people in the city, and soon everyone had enough to eat. It was just as Elisha said it would be.

Those four men were not selfish. They could have kept everything they found for themselves, but they didn't. What do you think God wanted them to do?

The Baby Prince

2 Kings 11:1–12:2

Joash was a baby prince. His
grandmother was evil. She wanted to
kill him so she could be queen. Joash's
aunt hid him in God's house until he was
seven years old.

116

Then soldiers came to God's house and got him. They made him king even though he was just a little boy. Joash ruled for 40 years in Jerusalem. He did what God said was right.

If you were made king today, what would you do first?

The Sun Goes Backward

2 Kings 20:1–11; Isaiah 38

Hezekiah was a good king. One day he got very sick. He knew he was going to die. He prayed and asked God to let him live a little longer. Then, to be sure that God had heard him, Hezekiah asked for the sun to go backward. He asked for the shadow that was at the bottom of the steps to go back up ten steps. And just as he asked, the shadow moved back up ten steps. And Hezekiah lived 15 more years.

For the sun to move backward would be as amazing as falling up instead of down. It was a miracle!

119

An Honest Man

Job 1:1–12

Job was an honest man who loved God.
He had a big family and was very rich.
Everything he did pleased God.

Then Satan, the enemy of God and man, went to God and said, "You are protecting Job from anything going wrong. That's why he obeys You." "All right," said God. "You can do anything to him except take his life."

Satan is very real. He doesn't like God, and he doesn't like us. But Job was about to find out that God is always with us.

When Bad Things Happen

Job 1:13–2:10

Awful things began to happen to Job.
His children died. His house fell down.
He got sores all over his body.

His cattle were taken away by robbers. His friends told him to turn away from God.

But Job never doubted that God loved him. Job was faithful to God, even in hard times.

When bad things happen, it doesn't mean God has forgotten about us. He's never far away in the bad times. And He wants us to continue to love and obey Him.

A Time for Everything

Ecclesiastes 3:1–8

There is a time for everything that happens in our lives. There are happy times and there are sad times.

124

There are times when we cry and times when we laugh.

There are times to hug and times not to hug.

There is a time to be silent and a time to speak.

A little bit of everything happens in our lives. The important thing is to stay close to God all the time.

A Message for King Ahaz

Isaiah 7:1–17; 9:2–7

God told the prophet Isaiah to take a message to a king named Ahaz. King Ahaz was in the family of King David. Isaiah told the king that someday God was going to send a child who would grow up to be a leader of all of God's people. He said that this person would be the Prince of Peace and would rule as King forever.

Who was Isaiah talking about? Today we know he was talking about Jesus, God's Son.

127

Writing on the Wall

Daniel 5:1–26

Daniel was one of God's people who was a slave in Babylon. One night the new king of Babylon gave a banquet. Suddenly a hand appeared and began writing on the wall something that no one could read. It was very scary!

The king asked Daniel to come and tell him what it meant. Daniel said it meant that God was angry with the king. And the kingdom of Babylon would be divided and given to two other countries, the Medes and Persians.

Daniel always lived for God no matter what anyone said. Let's see what happened to him.

Daniel Disobeys the King

Daniel 6:1-10

Daniel prayed three times every day. Some men in the new kingdom of the Medes and Persians wanted to get rid of Daniel. So they had the new king make a rule that people could only pray to the king. If someone broke the rule, he would be thrown into the lions' den.

But Daniel went to his house and got down on his knees and prayed to God just as he had always done.

Daniel knew that praying to God was more important than obeying the king's new rule.

A Den of Hungry Lions

Daniel 6:11-28

The men caught Daniel praying to God and told the king. The king was sad because he liked Daniel, but the king couldn't change the law. So Daniel was thrown into a den of hungry lions.

But wait! God sent an angel to close the mouths of the lions so they couldn't bite.

In the morning, the king came to see if God had saved Daniel, and sure enough, Daniel was just fine.

God saved Daniel. After being saved from the lions, do you think Daniel went on praying to God three times a day?

Jonah Runs Away

Jonah 1:1-3

"Go to Nineveh," God told a man named Jonah. "Tell them to stop their evil ways." Jonah got up, but he didn't go to Nineveh. He didn't like the people of that city, so he ran away.

Jonah went to the seashore. He got on a ship going the opposite direction from Nineveh. God saw what Jonah was doing.

**God always sees what we are doing.
He wants us to make good choices.**

A Big Storm!

Jonah 1:4–6

Jonah sailed away on the ship. When the ship was at sea, God sent a big storm. Waves pounded the ship. The sailors were very frightened of the storm.

The captain went down into the bottom of the ship and found Jonah sleeping. "Get up and pray to your God too," he said. "Maybe your God will save us!"

The captain and everyone prayed. They knew they needed help from somebody bigger than themselves.

Jonah Goes Overboard

Jonah 1:7–16

"Somebody has done something to cause this storm. Let's find out who it is," the sailors said. They decided the storm was Jonah's fault. "You're right. I ran away from God," Jonah told them. "Throw me into the sea. Then it will calm down."

So the sailors tossed Jonah overboard.
As soon as Jonah was in the water, the
sea became calm.

**You might think that would be the end of Jonah,
but it wasn't!**

Inside a Big Fish!

Jonah 1:17–2:9

Down, down into the swirling water went Jonah. Then *gulp!* Something swallowed him. Jonah was in the stomach of a big fish. God left him there to learn something important. It took three days and three nights.

Then Jonah prayed to God for help. He decided to do what God had told him to do.

It took a while for Jonah to catch on that he needed to obey God. Now, how was he going to get out of that fish?

Jonah Obeys God

Jonah 2:10–3:10

God had a plan. He spoke to that fish.
It swam up close to the beach and spit
Jonah out of its stomach onto dry land.

Right away God said to Jonah, "Get up and go to the great city of Nineveh. Say what I tell you to say." This time Jonah didn't argue. He obeyed. He jumped up and went straight to Nineveh.

Every time we disobey, we get in trouble.
What would be a better choice?

New
Testament

Where Is Jesus?

Luke 2:41-45

Every year Jesus' parents went to
Jerusalem to celebrate the Passover.
When Jesus was 12, they went as usual.
When Mary and Joseph started home, they
didn't see Jesus, but it was okay. They
thought Jesus was traveling with friends.

Late in the day they realized He wasn't with any of their friends. Mary and Joseph were very worried and hurried back to Jerusalem, looking for Him all along the way. They were afraid they had lost Jesus.

What are some places where Mary and Joseph might have looked for Jesus?

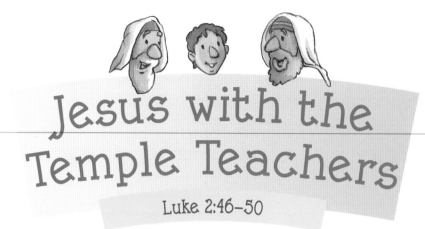

Jesus with the Temple Teachers

Luke 2:46–50

When Mary and Joseph found Jesus, He was in the Temple—a place where God's people went to worship. Twelve-year-old Jesus was talking with some teachers just like He was one of them. He asked them questions, and He answered theirs.

His mother had a question too. "Son, why did You stay behind? We were worried about You." Jesus said, "You should have known I must be where My Father's work is!"

That was a strange thing for Jesus to say. What do you think He meant?

Jesus Walks on the Water

Mark 6:45–53

One day Jesus told the followers who were His helpers to go to another city across the lake. He would come after a while. The helpers got into a boat. But that night in the middle of the lake, a strong wind came up. And the men had to work very hard to row the boat.

Then they saw something that frightened them more than the storm. They thought it was a ghost. But it wasn't a ghost. It was Jesus walking on the water. Jesus called to His helpers, "Don't be afraid." Then Jesus got into the boat, and the wind became calm.

If you had been in that boat, what would you have done?

A Very Short Man

Luke 19:1–10

Everywhere Jesus went,
there were crowds of people.
In one crowd there was a very
short man named Zacchaeus.
He wanted to see Jesus, but he
couldn't see over the crowd.
So he climbed a tree.

Jesus said, "Zacchaeus, come down
so we can go to your house today."
Zacchaeus hurried down and took Jesus
to his home. Zacchaeus wanted to do
good things. He told Jesus that he'd give
half of his money to the poor.

**Wouldn't it be exciting to have Jesus come to your
house? What would you do if Jesus came to see you?**

A Coin in a Fish

Peter, one of Jesus' helpers, came to tell
Jesus it was time for Him to pay taxes.
But Jesus and Peter didn't have any
money. Jesus knew just what to do. Jesus
told Peter, "Go to the lake and catch a
fish. You will find a coin in its mouth.
Use that coin to pay our taxes."

Aren't you glad Jesus always knows the best thing to do? Talk to Him about your problems.

A Blind Man Sees Again

Mark 10:46–52

Sick people followed Jesus everywhere. They wanted Him to heal them. One man who was blind heard that Jesus was walking by. He cried out, "Jesus, please help me!" People told the man to be quiet, but Jesus asked the man, "What would you like Me to do for you?"

The man said, "I want to see again." So Jesus healed the man's eyes. How happy the man was to see again!

Do you know someone who is sick? You could pray right now and ask Jesus to make them well.

A Very Poor Woman

Mark 12:41–44

Jesus was watching people put their money into the collection box at the Temple where God's people worshiped. Some rich people were very proud as they put in a lot of money.

Then a very poor woman came. In went her two small coins. *Plunk! Plunk!* Jesus told His closest followers, "This woman gave more than the rich people with many coins. The rich people gave only what they did not need, but this poor woman gave all the money she had."

Why do you think the woman gave God all the money she had?

Jesus Stops a Storm

Mark 4:35–41

Jesus and His followers got into a boat and set out across the lake. Jesus was so tired that He fell asleep. Soon a strong wind began to blow. Waves came over the sides of the boat. Everyone was very frightened.

160

They woke Jesus. "Help us, or we'll drown!" Jesus commanded the wind and waves to be still. The wind stopped, and there were no more waves coming into the boat. The lake became calm.

When you are frightened, what do you do?
Remember, Jesus is always there with you.
Just ask Him to help you. He will.

Jesus' Best Friends

Luke 10:38–42

One day Jesus went to visit His best friends Mary, Martha, and Lazarus. Martha was busy getting the meal ready. Mary was sitting and listening to Jesus talk.

Martha became angry and complained, "Jesus, don't You care that Mary left me to do all this work alone? Tell her to help me." Jesus said, "What Mary is learning from Me can never be taken away from her."

Why was Martha angry? What did Jesus tell her?

Jesus Brings Lazarus Back to Life

John 11:1–44

One day Lazarus got very sick. Mary and Martha sent a message to Jesus asking Him to come heal their brother. Even though Jesus loved His three friends, He waited two days to start the trip to see them, and Lazarus died before Jesus got there.

Martha and Mary said, "If You had come earlier, our brother wouldn't have died." Jesus was so sad He cried. Then He went to the tomb of Lazarus. He said, "Lazarus, come out!" And out came Lazarus, wrapped in the burial cloths. He was alive and well!

Sometimes when we ask Jesus for something, we have to wait—sometimes for a long time.

One Man Says Thank You

Luke 17:11–19

Ten men met Jesus as He was walking along a road. They didn't come close to Jesus because they had the horrible skin disease leprosy. They called out, "Please help us!" Jesus told them they were healed and sent them on their way.

As the men went on their way, the leprosy disappeared. Only one man came back. He bowed down to Jesus and thanked Him for what He had done.

We should remember to say thank you for what God has done for us. What has God done for you?

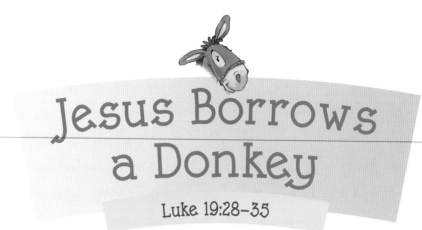

Jesus Borrows a Donkey

Luke 19:28–35

The first Passover happened when God's people left Egypt long ago. After that, God's people celebrated the Passover every year. One year Jesus and His closest followers went to Jerusalem to celebrate the Passover.

Before they got there, Jesus said to
His followers, "Go into town and find a
young donkey colt. Untie it and bring
it to Me. If anyone asks where you are
taking it, say, 'The Master needs it.'"
When the men got back with the donkey
colt, they spread their coats on
its back. Jesus climbed
on the colt.

Why do you suppose Jesus needed that donkey colt?

Jesus Rides Like a King

Luke 19:36–38; John 12:12–16

The donkey started to clippity-clop through the town. People came running. They threw their coats down for the donkey to walk on. They took palm branches and waved them in the air. "Praise God!" they shouted.

Some of them remembered the Scriptures that said, "Your king is coming . . . sitting on the colt of a donkey."

Why do you suppose they laid their coats down for the donkey to walk on?
Did they think Jesus was a king?

Jesus Shows How to Serve

John 13:1–17

Soon it was time for the Passover dinner. Jesus and His closest followers gathered in a big room. Jesus stood up, took off His coat, got some water in a wash bowl, and wrapped a towel around His waist.

Then He started washing His followers' feet. Jesus did this to teach His friends they were to serve one another.

Jesus was serving His followers to set a good example. What could you do to serve your brothers and sisters and parents?

The First Lord's Supper

Matthew 26:26–29; 1 Corinthians 11:23–25

While Jesus and His closest followers were eating the Passover dinner, Jesus took some bread and thanked God for it. He broke the bread apart and said, "Take this bread and eat it. Do this to remember Me."

174

Next He took a cup and said, "When you drink this juice of the grape, remember Me." Jesus knew this was His last meal with His followers because He was about to be killed. He wanted His followers to always remember Him.

Today in church we still eat bread and drink the juice of the grape to remember Jesus. We call this time of remembering *Communion* or *The Lord's Supper*.

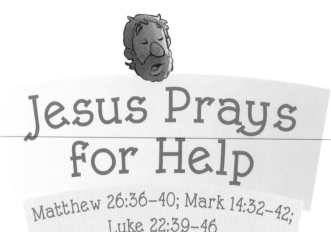

Jesus Prays for Help

Matthew 26:36–40; Mark 14:32–42; Luke 22:39–46

Jesus and His followers went straight from dinner to a quiet garden. Jesus wanted to pray and ask God to make Him strong for what was about to happen. He took three of His closest followers—Peter, James, and John—with him. Jesus asked them to wait and pray.

176

He went a little farther into the garden so that He could pray by Himself. It was very late, and the three men were very tired. They couldn't keep their eyes open to pray. Soon they were asleep. Jesus woke them twice, but they went back to sleep each time.

When we have tough things ahead of us, we need to pray and ask God to help us.

Jesus Is Arrested

Matthew 26:45–56; Luke 22:45–51; John 18:10–11

The third time Jesus woke His followers, He said, "We must go. Here comes the man who has turned against Me." Just then a big crowd carrying torches and clubs came into the garden. Judas, one of Jesus' followers, was with them. He kissed Jesus on the cheek. It was a signal to the guards to arrest Jesus.

Peter pulled out his sword and cut off the ear of one guard. Jesus told Peter to put the sword away. Then He healed the guard's ear.

You might think the crowd would let Jesus go after He healed the man's ear. Well, they didn't. They arrested Him and took Him away.

Pilate Questions Jesus

Luke 22:52–23:25

Lots of people loved Jesus, but there were many who didn't like Him at all. After Jesus was captured in the garden, He was taken to the house of the high priest, then to Pilate, the Roman governor of Judea.

All night the rulers asked Jesus if He was God's Son. They did not believe that He was. Finally Pilate said that he didn't think Jesus was guilty. But the people who hated Jesus kept yelling until Pilate decided that Jesus had to die on a cross.

Jesus told everyone that He was God's Son, and that made some people very angry. But even if they didn't believe it, He was still God's Son.

Jesus Is Killed on a Cross

Matthew 27:27–40; Mark 15:25–27

Pilate's soldiers took Jesus and put a crown of thorns on His head and made fun of Him. Then they led Jesus out of the city to a place called Golgotha to be killed on a cross.

At nine o'clock in the morning, the soldiers nailed Jesus to the cross. They also put two robbers beside Jesus, one on the right and one on the left.

The day God's Son died on the cross was a sad day. But God had a wonderful plan. Keep reading and you'll see what it was.

A Dark Day

Matthew 27:45–54; Luke 23:44–49; Hebrews 9

While Jesus was on the cross, the land became dark from noon until three o'clock. Then Jesus died, and there was a big earthquake.

When the earth shook, the thick curtain in the Temple between the Holy Place and the Most Holy Place ripped from top to bottom. Now people could see inside the Most Holy Place. Before, only the High Priest got to see inside. When the soldiers at the cross saw what happened when Jesus died, they knew He really was the Son of God!

Jesus died because He loved us. He died so that our sins could be forgiven. Let's tell Him right now that we love Him for what He did on the cross.

Jesus Is Laid in a Tomb

Luke 23:50–56

A rich man, named Joseph of Arimathea, had a new tomb where he had planned to be buried. He took Jesus' body from the cross and put it in his own empty tomb.

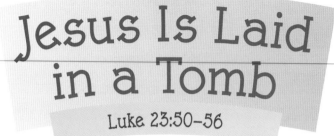

Joseph and Jesus' friends wrapped
His body in strips of linen and laid it
carefully in the tomb. Roman soldiers
came to guard the tomb. They rolled a
huge stone over the door and sealed
it in a way that would show if anyone
tried to move the stone.

**Everyone thought that since Jesus was dead,
they would never see Him again.
They were in for a big surprise!**

A Big Surprise

Matthew 28:1–10

The day after Jesus was buried was a holy day, so His friends had to stay home. Then very early on Sunday morning, the first day of the week, the women went back to the tomb. It was the third day since Jesus died.

When the women got there, they couldn't believe their eyes. The stone had been rolled away! An angel of God was sitting on the stone! The soldiers were so frightened they were like dead men.

How do you think those women at the tomb felt when they saw the angel?

Jesus Is Alive!

Matthew 28:5–8; Luke 24:9–12

The angel said, "Don't be afraid. Jesus is alive." Those women were as happy as they could be! They ran to find other friends of Jesus.

190

Some of Jesus' friends didn't believe what the women said. But everything the women said was true. Jesus was alive! He had risen from death.

How long is forever? Jesus promised He would come back to life . . . and He did. Jesus is alive today and will be forever.

Jesus Eats Dinner with Two Friends

Luke 24:13–32

Two of Jesus' friends were walking along the road, and Jesus joined them. These two people didn't know it was Jesus who was walking with them. But they liked talking with this man.

They invited Him to have dinner at their house. Jesus came, and while He was thanking God for the food, the friends realized the man was Jesus. Then Jesus disappeared.

After Jesus was raised from the dead, He could appear and disappear. What would you do if Jesus suddenly appeared here?

Jesus Appears to a Room Full of Friends

Luke 24:33-49

One night Jesus appeared in a room where many of His friends were gathered. He told them to tell their family and friends and neighbors and even strangers that He is alive.

He told them to share everything He had taught them. They were to tell the people in Jerusalem first, but then they were to tell people everywhere. Jesus told them to wait in Jerusalem until God sent them a special gift of power from heaven.

Whom do you know that would like to hear all about Jesus' love?

Jesus Goes to Heaven

Luke 24:50–53; Acts 1:6–11

Jesus led His followers a little way out of town. Jesus prayed for His followers, and while He was praying, He started to rise up into heaven. Then a cloud hid Him from His followers.

As everyone was standing there staring up into heaven, two angels appeared and said, "Jesus has been taken away from you and into heaven. He will come back in the clouds, just like He went away."

Remember the gift that God was going to send? Keep reading and see what happened.

God's Spirit Comes to Help

Acts 2:1–4

After Jesus went back to heaven, His friends and helpers were praying together in a big room. Suddenly something amazing happened.

198

First it sounded as if a huge wind were blowing. Next flames of fire flickered over every person's head. Then God's Spirit came, and everyone began to speak in different languages. This was the gift from God that Jesus had promised His followers.

Jesus' friends were happy. God's Spirit had come to live with them and to help them.

Everyone Hears
and Understands

Acts 2:5–42

The night that God's Spirit came to Jesus'
followers, there were people from many
countries in Jerusalem. These people
spoke different languages.

When they heard Jesus' friends praying, they went to see what the noise was all about. They found Jesus' friends telling about the great things God had done.

But they were all surprised to hear it in their own language. "What does this mean?" they asked.

God's Holy Spirit still helps those
who follow Jesus today.

A Beggar at the Temple

Acts 2:43–3:10

After that day when the Holy Spirit first came, Jesus' followers began to do many miracles, telling people about God's love and how Jesus had come to save them. One afternoon Peter and John went to the Temple. A man who couldn't walk sat there begging for money. Peter looked at him and said, "I don't have any money, but I do have something else I can give you: By the power of Jesus Christ from Nazareth— stand up and walk!" Up jumped the man. His feet and ankles were now strong.

Do you know someone who is sick? Now is a good time to pray and ask Jesus to help them.

Philip Meets an Ethiopian

Acts 8:26–31

Philip was another one of Jesus' followers. He was busy telling people about Jesus when an angel spoke to him. "Go out on the road," the angel said. Along came a very important man from Ethiopia riding in his chariot. He was reading from the book of Isaiah.

Philip ran alongside the chariot and said, "Do you understand what you are reading?" No, the man didn't understand. He stopped the chariot and invited Philip to ride in the chariot and explain what the book meant.

God looks for people, like Philip, who are ready to do what He asks.

Philip Baptizes the Ethiopian

Acts 8:32-40

Philip explained the Scripture passage the man was reading. It was all about Jesus. The man asked, "Why don't I get baptized?" The Ethiopian man believed in Jesus, and he wanted to be baptized.

So they stopped the chariot, and Philip baptized him. Then God needed Philip in another place, and *whoosh!* Just like that, Philip was gone.

When we do what God asks of us, we don't know what will happen next. We just need to be ready for whatever it is.

Peter in Jail

Acts 12:1–18

One day mean King Herod threw Peter, one of Jesus' followers, in jail. The king had 16 soldiers guard Peter so he couldn't get away. That night an angel came into Peter's cell. "Hurry! Get up!" the angel said. "Follow me." Peter thought he must be dreaming . . . but he wasn't. The chains fell off his hands, and the angel led him past the guards. When they came to the iron gate of the prison, it swung open on its own, and Peter was free.

God is always stronger than anything that can happen to us. We have to trust that He will always do what's best for us.

209

New Heaven and Earth

Revelation 21

One of the biggest promises God ever
made was that we will live with Him
in heaven forever. He said that there
would be a new heaven and a new earth
and we would get a new body—one that
won't get old but will live forever.

In the new heaven, no one will ever be sad again. No one will ever die again. The streets will be made of gold, and there will be gates of pearl. Everything will be more beautiful than anything you can imagine. And best of all, Jesus will be there. We will be with Him forever.

What is the most beautiful thing you have ever seen? Heaven will be a thousand times more beautiful.

God Keeps His Promises

God will give you what he promised,
because you are his child.

Galatians 4:7

Bringing the Bible to life for your little ones with **Read and Share**®

Packed with 200 stories, *The Read and Share® Bible* is sure to win the hearts of little ones and give them a strong Bible foundation.

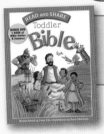

The Read and Share® Toddler Bible offers 40 stories plus a 60-minute DVD for even the littlest of God's children.

The Read and Share® DVD Bible series builds a foundation in knowing God's Word in young minds. Collection includes 52, 3-minute Bible stories in bold, bright animation.

Straight from the pages of the popular *Read and Share® Bible*, The Jesus Series walks children though the birth, life, death and resurrection of Christ.

Learn more about *Read and Share®*!
www.TommyNelson.com